WONDERINGS

BY KENNETH PATCHEN

AFLAME AND AFUN OF WALKING FACES

AN ASTONISHED EYE LOOKS OUT OF THE AIR

A SHEAF OF EARLY POEMS

A SURPRISE FOR THE BAGPIPE-PLAYER

BECAUSE IT IS

BEFORE THE BRAVE

BUT EVEN SO

CLOTH OF THE TEMPEST

DOUBLEHEADER

FABLES & OTHER LITTLE TALES

FIRST WILL & TESTAMENT

GLORY NEVER GUESSES

HALLELUJAH ANYWAY

HURRAH FOR ANYTHING

MEMOIRS OF A SHY PORNOGRAPHER

ORCHARDS, THRONES & CARAVANS

OUT OF THE WORLD OF PATCHEN

PANELS FOR THE WALLS OF HEAVEN

PICTURES OF LIFE AND DEATH

POEMSCAPES

POEMS OF HUMOR & PROTEST

RED WINE & YELLOW HAIR

SEE YOU IN THE MORNING

SELECTED POEMS

SLEEPERS AWAKE

THE COLLECTED POEMS OF KENNETH PATCHEN

THE DARK KINGDOM

THE FAMOUS BOATING PARTY

THE JOURNAL OF ALBION MOONLIGHT

THE LOVE POEMS OF KENNETH PATCHEN

THE TEETH OF THE LION

THEY KEEP RIDING DOWN ALL THE TIME

TO SAY IF YOU LOVE SOMEONE

TRANSLATIONS FROM THE ENGLISH

WHEN WE WERE HERE TOGETHER

WONDERINGS

WONDERINGS

KENNETH PATCHEN

A NEW DIRECTIONS BOOK

Manufactured in the United States of America.
First published clothbound and as ND Paperbook 320 in 1971.
Published simultaneously in Canada by McClelland &
Stewart Limited.

New Directions Books are published for James Laughlin
by New Directions Publishing Corporation,
333 Sixth Avenue, New York 10014.

for Miriam

But if your precious
illusion should turn out
not to be real where then
will you leap, my little flea

Any

who live
stand
alone in
one
place   together

And it is true, it is true
I saw the ships
beautiful as ever
maiden singing

in a dream

Yes,

I saw the ships   but
they were all sailing
away

To Whomever
These village fires
Still have meaning

O may your own most secret
& most beautiful Animal of Light
Come safely to you

The Great Fly Fleet

Steaming into the Sunset
The tossing hair of the Sea-Fellow
Turning the color of scarlet sugar
Under their sticky little keels
   "Oh Captain! Hey there, Captain dear...
The Big Wet One, again he threatens to scratch."
"So-oo? Up with them anchors then, you dopes!
   — Besides, how many times must I tell you?!
We've got to get out of this world!"

O honor the bird
That opened the word
That found the world
That Love might live

O choose the wonder
That knelt on the water
That sun & wind made move
And Love O it shall flame
Though darkness quell
Each and every name

ALLLIGHT SAVING TIME

Turn your clocks
sideways
to the hour
where
no- body
can get a good clean
shot at you

Binding the quiet into chalky sheaves
I do not forget to pack spirit-moss
And lonely isles of hasty leaves
Into these "boxes" which will toss
Upon the sea until next Wednesday
When some good soul knowing them mine
Shall bring them back without a word—
And inside I'll find sixteen baby foxes
Sleeping at the breast of a great milk-white bird

IN BACK OF

EVERY REALLY THOUGHTFUL CHICKEN

Is some motherly egg or other

Smiling chalkily (although bald)

~ Until it gets popped into a pan

Or mauled by a train or marauding elk

But from the leg of that hickory tree

A dappled little pelican beams down on me

Believe

that
apples
could talk

if they had *a mind too*

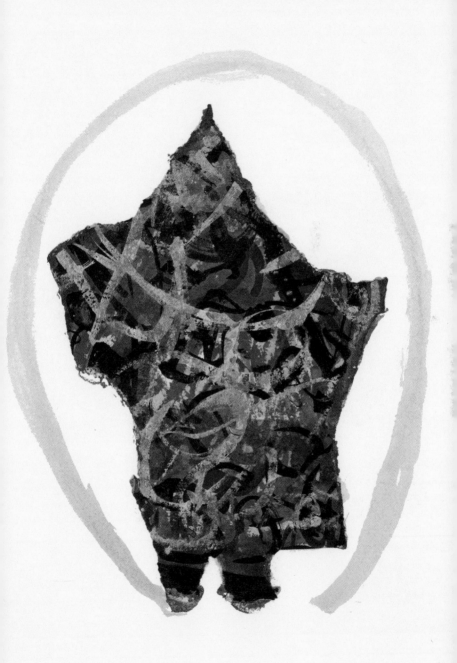

WHAT INDEED!

If I am Higgs and he is Humberson
If I am that rich and he's without a cent
Then why can't I at least go down
To my Aunt Lettie's on the seashore
And use one of the spare rooms.
Perhaps the one with the disappearing floor
Until, say, Delia or Joan can get there,
Or until so me chance wader bobs up?
What's the good of being Higgs otherwise

O "listen" is like an elephant
Who stalks the woods at night
& with his mole-soft & curling trunk
Touches all the stars with light
& written on his nobly gentle sides
Are the names of trees & fields & men
Of where we shall go tomorrow
And of what it will be like then

KEEP IT

Keep it in the hither
It will gleam
Keep it from their weather
It's your ice cream
Hide it in the queen's room
O don't you be mean
Hide it in that cleanest kingdom
Where it won't ever be seen
'Cause, brother, that's your only ice cream

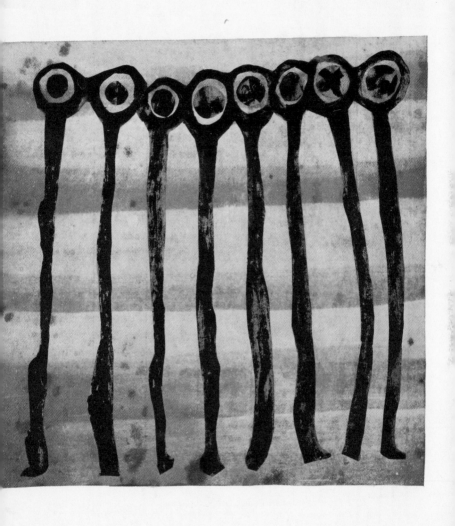

The Broom Of Bells

Has swept a path for her

From village windows
The voices of children
Fill her name with cool flowers

Thus at sweet evening

Welcome we this lovely one

Since in the
patient eye
of mouse & swan & fly
all our plagues
& conflagrations glide
as dust upon
the uncaring wind

If You Can Lose Your Head

When all aground you
Are busy clothing bares
Then we may let you in
To greet a rather different kind of King

This is "the Animal That Walks Sitting Down"

It is not an animal you can tire easily

In addition I am looking up at the sky

And if a voice suddenly shouts down out of that cloud

I'm sure it will most certainly say

Good luck everybody!

What a lovely morning!

T h e

The nose of morning is bleeding a bit, my love.

Oh no—not enough to worry about.

but see the pink stain on its handerchief snagged there upon the willows Yes! I'd love some more coffee

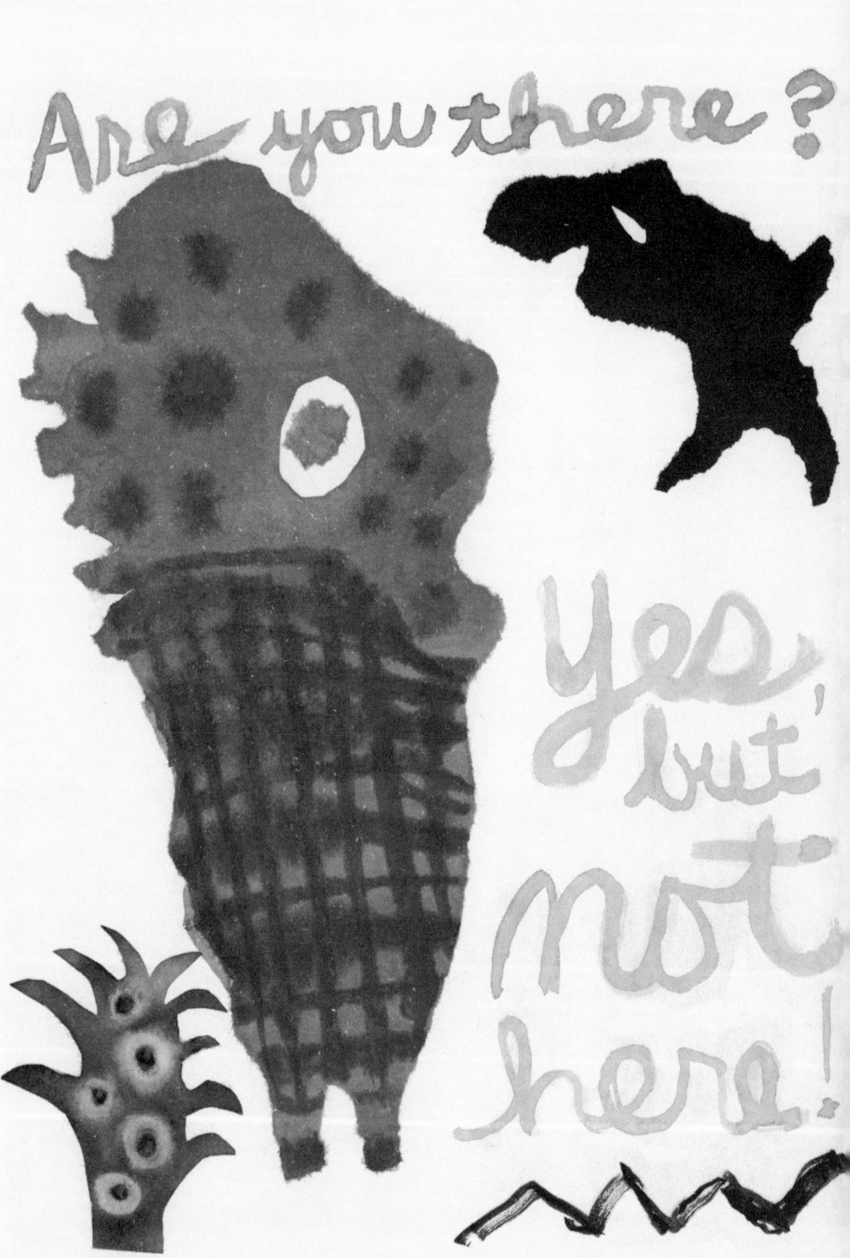
Are you there?
Yes, but not here!

The Moment

Before the girl picking field daisies

Becomes the girl picking field daisies

There is a moment of some complexity

I see again that Giraffe-of-Sofas
Who at morning leaves snippets of old films
In his grateful and explosive wake
Here are fishes with smiling human faces

Canoeing along banks lined with green-backed bushes
Here are questioning little fellows (λ λ λ λ λ)
Riding upside down in stiff-collar wagons

Here from a rainbarrel the limp ear of Wednesday
Dangles beside a porcupine bouquet

Let us rejoice,
then,
remembering
all
the grand  
(but deserved)
things
that some-
how never managed to come our way

HOUSE on HORSEBACK

The drover follows along
Not to earn
    the opal-encrusted
        whistle
        promised him

But only to be within an ace of coming through
What he hasn't the least idea of
    It's just that it has
        such a pretty lilt to it

GARRITY
THE GAMBLING
MAN
... GROWN OLD

Once Memphis Grandee of the Quick-Chill Deck
Now at rainy 3 a.m. out of Dallas T
And all the pretty queens have long since gone hagging
All the brave jack-o-knights have been shunted down slack's lane
O Garrity— once the best of all the river's best —
This is what it comes to then
A sick old man in a smelly daycoach
Riding nowhere through the night
Without a lousy dime to his name

TO "RUN THE CROWN

You go down a little below all pride
Where on the bursting, emerald air
Salamanders ride & pretty periwinkles hide
On the bent steps of Moon Inn
All considerably begun that's modestly done
So only moving in seashell & turtle's sleep
You soon lie down on a sinless bed
And understand what understanding never meant
And why the Bride of Mountains may not weep

O quietly the SUN-MAN sits
    In his chair above the world.
Here the old men are blundering liars,
And the young men are cheated of life;
But the golden hands caress all alike:
        O a hundred thousand no ones
            Proclaiming life a fraud—
        A hundred hundred thousand no ones
With just themselves to blame, not God.

The words that speak up from the mangled bodies of human beings

This is the fallout that covers everything on earth now

QUICK THINKER

Someone has left a wave
In front of the barn.
It grabs hold of the cow.
Poor Grandma has to dismount.
Her skirt gets caught.
The sky catches on fire.
The wave goes to work
And soon puts it out.
Someone sure used his bean!

The monument-maker is little fellow
He could use a hot supper
Instead he goes, in he asks the real estate man
"What you got about this size
With a great big forest here
And maybe a great huge big forest right there"
(About the size of fifty Pennsylvanias!)
"Pay? <u>Me</u> pay! Why, hell
All I want it for is to set up
A love-size portrait of a butterfly on"

From "the Teakettle Suggestion"
A man is led to good in small elevators
Soon villages and what amusing acrobats
When you depend on it
Harmony of wave's share & Old Shirttail
(My favorite cloud)
Now definitely one outranks none
On no account let them glue any generals on.
Not while you & I are in charge around here

The Little
Bug Angel

He bangs his wings on the table!
Still no service!
What's the matter that waiter!
Wow! smell that roast beff!
Ah! he takes out a stick of dynamite—
Brrr-uump! That should teach them!
But nothing happens!
Of course, obviously, the dynamite of an angel that size
Does not (fortunately) pack very much of a wallop.

IT'S

ALWAYS
TOO SOON
OR
TOO LATE

Fact is,

the train
don't come
on time
for
nobody

except
those who
should walk
all the way
to hell on their
own backs

All things are

all things
True?
And if
not,
how not..
Then, my
little two-legged flea,
name me one
single thing
that is not

all
things!
Eh?

An Old Lady named Amber Sam

Piltched a REVERSE-STRIPE Zebra

Off a Stalled MovingVan

But since the Zee had no Built-In Spoon

Any Soup she gave him lacked All-Jiggable Tune

So she put on an Old Pair of Baggy Pants

And snuck Quietly out to a NEIGHBOR'S CAR

AND shifted BOTH of its Headlights onto the REAR-Bumper

COUNSEL FOR THE OFFENSE

Who gives his uncle a gear
For turning marbles into bears,
Shall always come when very near;
But who gives his aunt a stick
That will of bison make storks,
Must always loaf unless he works.
So if you wish really to thrive,
Act warmly toward that ball you throw—
For Summer's best jive is not snow,

Behind in his rent
Too tired even
 to lie down
His best tin crown
 badly dented

While his subjects
 just loll around
munching rusty old
bottle tops

Certainly not
 much

to pred   icate

A really driving
 reign on

THE
KING
OF
LOG-
OONA

Unless there are flowers
And years that begin in Spring,
Unless the greatest sea
Is made of little waters
And life is least what it seems
Then I may not love thee

Which of us
is not

flesh?

Last

and first,
in that
common cause.

Beyond

this— I would like to be able
to say... to say mos

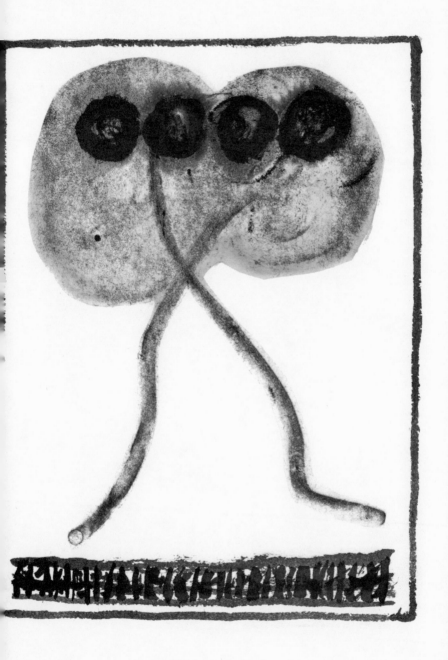

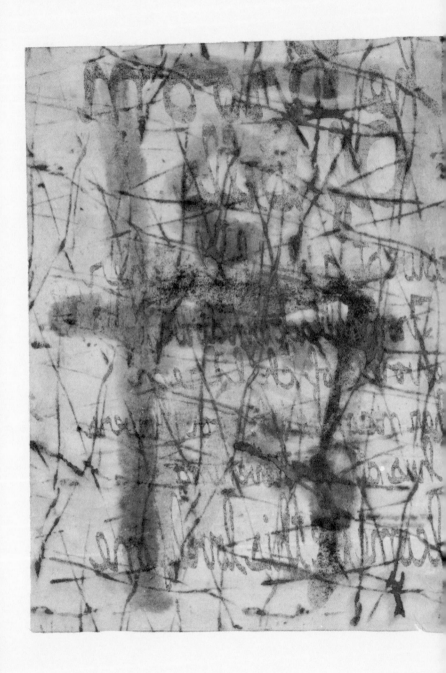

Who are you
Watching out of the water lily
Watching out of the oak tree
Daughter of the linnet's waking
Draughtsman of the tempest's oath
Who are you
Watching out of the wounded fawn
Watching out of the frolicking hare
O Designer of what awesome tidings

Sleeper Under The Tree

O shape the pillow
And shape the bell
Where no flower darkens
Where no thought weeps
Where no blade flashes
And no wave leaps
Where no hag is waiting
Where all beds are sweet
And where all our coats are unstained, my lord

The Question Is

What you doing there
On that dirty coalbarge,
You little puff-cheek rhino?
You can't be a prisoner,
You're sitting on the captain.
You can't even be very lonesome,
Not and play that kinda slidehorn!
Maybe it's you should be asking me
How come I'm over here, huh?

It's really lousy taste to live in a world like this

TIGER CONTEMPLATING A CAKE

Somebody had to be around here
Quite a while before he could

Build up to

figuring on a way

To excuse time spent

on this bauble

Why, with a   little more trouble

He could be getting out a nice refreshing wildebeest-blood cola

Which didn't require no deposit for the bottle either

Why you running, pal?

You'll be all tuckered out by
the time you get where you're goin'.
Where I'm goin'? Do you reckon
I'd be blurrin' ground like this
if I had me any place to go.

Do you think that somebody will find us in time?

Yeah, I'm afraid so. That's the one thing they're bloody good at.

Waiting at the bathhouse while a duck is

already having a fine swim for himself below

Seems different

now they've taken the

rose-colored penguins off this page

They'd slide up here laughing & having lots of fun like everything was going to turn out fine — against the law, I guess

Arrival

of

the

mailorder

dog

there's no
point saying
anything
except what
you
can't

Take your own hand and lead yourself
into the unneeding
place-of-you

Glory
never guesses

Ah! cherish the Smiling Moose
Who heaps basketsful of forgetmenots
Upon the blushing little beavers
And gaily dons gay-checkered knickers
To cycle off to cozify his Lovely Ella
With a rupple-dupple-dobbie-o
With a sneggle-keggle-owego
So you get with it too, dad
Love's worth all the sad

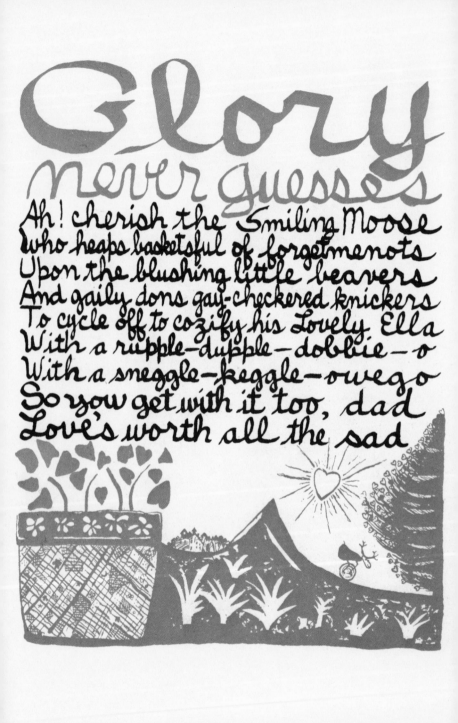

A SURPRISE FOR THE BAGPIPE PLAYER

Who expected no one would notice
That he'd gone home

Without even bothering to care

None
can
leave
where
he's
going

May all that have
life be

deliver-
ed from
evil-
willed
suffering.

Hindu invocation

"Blessedness is not the
reward
of virtue,
it is
virtue itself"
Spinoza

"Everyman is me,

I am his brother. No man is my enemy. I am Everyman and he is in and of me.

This is my faith, my strength, my deepest hope and my only belief."